Aversions

DEVIN JOHNSTON : AVERSIONS

OMNIDAWN : RICHMOND, CALIFORNIA : 2004

Omnidawn Publishing
Richmond, California
www.omnidawn.com
(800) 792-4957

ISBN 1-890650-16-1

Cover: Brian Calvin, "Wildflower" (2003)
courtesy of the artist and Corvi-Mora, London
Cover design by Quemadura
Text design by the author

Cataloging-in-Publication Data appear
at the end of the book

Contents

Leave off
the dedication,
which so suggests
something willed—
the insect's-eye
inspiration
of cut glass
we admired
but could not want.
The fine, smudgy
print at the back
of our weekly
declaring, William,
we miss you—
is California so mild?;
the fresh forgetting
of the unremembered;
the paper trail
of a freighted
marriage gone south:
all these are true
to poetry,
but let's leave off
perverse accounts
and live aside.

We go on loving those we have loved in other forms, or else we begin to cherish in other forms those we should have cherished in the past. Nothing changes, everything is transformed.

VIOLETTE LEDUC

Ghost

When talking to myself,
I take a tone I've learned

from you—not of boyish charm,
but probing and severe—

to say, *some things are clear
and some withdrawn from sight.*

A cyclist is only such
while seated on a bike,

a sleeper while asleep.
These forms are only forms

fulfilled, as you are now
no more than this—a tone.

In an Orchard

Shades of Gram
somatic code

I sense some strain
of you in what

I am—or did
in turning down

a cell path
choked with vines

from a relict rose
or metal vetch

impediments

of what I own
to what I owe

the shadow of
a seed unfurled

I was a wolf
and not a lamb

as your thoughts
turned to mine

ensconced in pulp
I found you

hard but not

so difficult
to understand

Character

The insistence on order among toys
reflected a larger disorder.

Sunlight on the rifle's sight
entailed a world outside

and preceded my character,
which I thought more likely

stalking behind my shoulder,
making a nuisance of itself

out of what I knew
without my knowledge.

On a slip-up, among strangers,
I took leave of my senses

and called a sudden halt—on the chance
it might lurch past and into view.

Aversion

The characters who populate
your waking life tend to possess
some glaring flaw—specific rage
or weakness which, demonstrative,
becomes their essence—so refined
with each retelling of their lives
that little shames, and baby-talk,
and hallowed scars from distant wars
have burned away. As Red-Cap proves—
your torturer in Flint that June,
who never doffed his epithet
and never caught you by surprise
so upper-case was his approach:
a red cap floating in the crowd,
a red cap at the barbershop,
arcade, or park. Your Red-Cap's now
an Ovid-bird—some flicker, finch,
or cardinal—transfixed in endless chase.

We need to make a sacrifice
to keep such knowledge from ourselves.
My friend, perform aversions!—smear

the doors with pitch, the floors with blood,
and chew on spine-tipped buckthorn strips
to fend them off—those spirits who
would collar us, stare in our eyes,
and then—as Slinger says—*describe.*

Piazza Dante

The conjurer deployed
a grain upon the stroller's hood
and turned his rubber knobs

toward the sky: a pigeon dropped
to scutter round the heads
of people in the square, who kept

still, but laughed as it hopped
to the apron and cut
its single-note complaint—

fierce red eye searching.

Dark Wood

Dashing through the station
in the final collapse
of time, I'm already dead.

It is all one where I begin:
at Niagara, where we never were,
or the Casentino,
Dante's wood, in which
the tangled limbs of Guelphs
lay thick as leaves
that strow the brooks.

Beneath a canopy of lime
which darkens the Daewoo's
windshield, we glide
through dictionaries
in search of mouflon.

One week married: *if, then.*
Wherever I start,
I'm lost to the language
and still putting paper to pen.

Dead

Some find it dangerous
to analyze the dead:

they shut a collie in
the cote, then find him gone—

or else, the blackest plum
proves bitter on the tongue;

an unequated remnant
lodges in the head.

When venturing abroad,
they tilt each name and date

against their silhouettes,
and looking up, take aim:

the landscape loses depth,
collapsing near and far

as plumbing groans when taps
are turned, emitting air.

The bed is hard, the room
is cold, and some have found

the dead, though well-attuned,
are slow to understand.

February

Pitch-black
doors detain
a darker fact:

we know
of no wide sky
to award,
but ward off
those we've known
too well.

Avert your eyes:

someone takes
a metal crate
of apples
from the trunk—
but not for us.

Each night
we undertake
a voyage of
avoidance.

The Roman World

Yew and eye
    and eye and yew
soak up the dark
    while you are gone.
This shade unfurled
    from root to bough
was planted here
    when I was born.

Within its reach
    I shut my eye
to eye of day
    and day's return
as goldeneye
    in summer seek
extremities
    of arctic sun.

By day endure
    Saint Augustine,
October hail,
    the falling Dow;

at night the eye
    revolves in dreams
of you and me
    and me and you.

One

Like Odysseus under the ram
you cling beneath your lovers—
seeking to pass for them
by pressing close, supine.

Amongst the tangled curls,
who could tell one from the other?
Not I, who wade against the waves
with darkened eye and darkened mind.

Early Spring

AFTER HORACE

The hardest of winters will crack
    at the tap of spring and milder systems:
performance yachts
    are winched from dry-dock storage;
chafed by confinement,
    the amateur botanist hates his apartment,
and city parks no longer shine with frost.

Venus ascends through the elms
    as the moon swings closer
and teens entwine
    their fingers as they ramble,
sandals abandoned; a night-
    shift employee waves her scanner,
restocking surge suppressors
    of summer lightning.

Now is the time to relax
    with a puff of grass to tangle thoughts
with flowers, which float
    above the thawing earth.
On the shadowy paths
    of the graveyard, it's time to burn
some useless sacrifice to wildness.

Colorless death will descend
    on Division's tattered kiosk
or Board of Trade, regardless.
    You've been lucky, David:
hope for the future's restricted—
    the longest of lives is short.
Night and half-remembered
    forms are closing in—

a thin and emotionless heaven.
    Within its walls,
no joke of yours will ripple
    through the darkness
(lending a wonderful curl
    to McPherson's lip, for whom
the boys now burn, and girls will soon catch fire).

Distant Warnings

AFTER CATULLUS

Trembling veil, my limit—
whether I plumb the Marianas Trench
as waves of doubt thunder
miles above;

or brush a stand of birch
with sheaths of rain, or net
a white noddy adrift
on beds of kelp;

whether and whither the mind
wanders in dreamy disquietude,
asleep of a prairie noon
as buckboards creak,

prepared to risk the latitudes
of chance and trance—
to the Querent convey
a warning word:

awake to the world, the skin
is supple and resilient,
susceptible to stroke
or sudden heat.

But with a glance this veil
will fall as when a flower falls
glanced by the iron edge
of a passing plow.

Between Buildings

Haunting this world.

By necessary law.

Some said hush.

Memory must be admitted.

Souls that drag a burden.

Tell all done and felt.

The very shade leans out.

Phantom Dwelling

FOR STAN BRAKHAGE

I

Since last I wrote
   my little bird
      has turned into a cat,

horizon hedge
   to bauhaus block
      since feather touched the page.

The names I knew
   have all been struck
      from sidewalks marked in proof,

and consequence
   divorced from act—
      as thought divorced from sense—

since last I put
   my burnished steel
      engraver to the plate.

II

In the first autumn downpour,
    nettles disperse;
smooth calculi
    scatter in the flood.

Particles far smaller
    than those of surging rain
outstrip them in mobility,
    moved by a slighter impetus.

Thought is light—
    its fabric swayed
by mere images
    of smoke and mist.

A puddle of finger's depth
    formed in hollows
between the highway's cracks
    offers to the eye

a downward view
　　of such scope
as the vertiginous sky
　　that yawns above.

The velocity of surface film
　　accelerates at night;
painted cellulose acetate
　　smothers the steady light.

III

In anticipation of the night,
Mimi arches
                against the screen
while Red circles the rug.

Light softens,
and the sky begins to snow;
lacquered larches click
against the glass.

Phone lines crackle,
breaking up
the slow refrain

I just don't know.
I just don't know.

IV

Though living in my head,
I would speak my mind—

my mind has changed /
I've changed my mind.

I stand behind
a wall of flame

which some have called
screen memory

and others call
the hollows;

in back of which
amongst the summer trees

a sudden flock alights—
something to count on.

Cat

When light has come
    I stalk the flies, or seek
among the folds of down
    caloric heat.
       Quite delicate
and full of doubts, I scent a change
from what was here—a foreign tinge.

What reason could
    I give, what would I give
to reason? The smoothest manners hide
    some furtive love:
       I know—and have
thus arched my back of static fur
against a boot from out-of-doors.

Lost Wallet

Obstinate substance
      survives the river,
            survives the astringent

tannery, kitsch,
      dead smelt,
            and silverfish.

Surviving pleasure,
      its suck
            leaves us thinner

and each bank
      counselled as to
            its flow—

concretized to move
      more swiftly, elsewhere
            distressed to slow.

Posts of pale
      duck-egg
            drift past

as money skirrs
     the tacky tar
         where once unfurled

a Bourbon flag.
     We have brought
         everything to market.

Ice

Wait and watch
        as ice disobeys
                the water

forms evolve
        to violate
                every essence

changing past
        recall or projection,
                shedding

calf from berg
        and bringing to heel
                affection.

Dry Star

When Mister Glass has set to work,
you'd need a wax pencil
to circle where the cracks had been.

But I could tell of times
the vacuum failed, or bull's-eye
from a home-run hit
survived meticulous repair.

Taipei expo, early June,
eleven years ago:

the fluorescent lamp
that cured our diamond resin
died, and left us in a sweat.

Since sunlight is another
agent, Araki and I
dragged our demonstration pane
beside the rooftop pool:

buffeting winds from the Pescadores
buckled plexiglass,
and what late light there was
lit up capillaries, chips,
and a cloud of fingerprints.

That's when I switched to Dry Star—
and never once looked back.

Mars-Lumograph

Pencils
scratch—their shadows
rejoin scuds of day.

Itches
neither prosperous
nor useful hatch
current and star index
on trapper keepers,

sharpen
seedlings planted by
dead men, or tap

graphite
lead on teeth:
in their midst, what to say?

Black Balloons

At seven, thought balloons
ascend through trees,
each endless surface lit
by Betelgeuse.

Working nights, I wake
to the roll and clap
of skateboards—wave on wave
of debris in a dry bed.

With nothing much in mind
I wash my face
and read a letter from
Brazil. Outside

the dogman holds a blade
of grass between
his thumbs: its whistle penetrates
both brick and bone.

An awning snaps;
exhaust pursues a bus
emblazoned with cartoons
of singing cats

down crowded streets,
and through the minimum of space
from window sill to sash
a thought escapes.

Doubtful Weather

Cyclone system,
you star in a film—

disturbing
elements excite

a false rapport
in various substances:

shadows shrivel
in the park,

metal turns to ice,
and plastic bags to birds.

With hook and eye
unhooked,

a shutter knocks
against my thoughts—

to punctuate
and interrupt.

With a rush
of wings

a dark-green shade
descends;

and then it goes
away again.

Camels

FOR TOM RAWORTH

What reveals the daily space
   of the head hollowed out—
a concave bubble
   on the surface of water—

as smoking on film
delights in the medium's
   own properties
of light and opacity?

It is something we cross
   the shifting sands
to extinguish—days,
the rate of burning leaves.

Blank Blues

I

End of day
arrives with much
    left undone:
the galleys still unsent,
the table still uncleared.

Lazy wren
which builds its nest
    on the ground,
what is the gutter's height
against that great remove?

II

I sense an allegory taking shape
out there—in common sense—beyond the thermo-pane:

Clemente High (so aptly named, just now
a truant puff of smoke drifts into view)
has lost its flags, and managed to achieve
an achromatic consensus of concrete and snow.

What is that *chirr-rrk-rrk*—some accidental species,
or New Connecticut Grinder, ratcheting
the graphite point toward cursive clarity—?

III

Blown speaker.

Dirty broom.

The things I never fix,
my mind fixed on

the talk at large
of rise and reputation.

IV

Having fallen out of friendship

regarder means to look

the midnight student
                glances up

from *Vous et Moi,*
        a grammar book:

Goodbye to Illinois.

Los Angeles

The Colorado River flows—
sans silt—through fluted taps
in Universal City. Saturn nears.

Beneath millennia and shale
a riot growth of giant fern
and brontosauri decompose—
but through the auspices
of wildcats, blaze
                    in incandescent beads
along a sliding mirror: long extinct,
their ghosts reticulate the hills
and hulks of studios—an Oz
of local urgencies.

Beneath the moon, emotions are
but vectors, dragging
                    distant objects near.

As daikon sputters on an open flame,
the owner of Pagoda Inn

cradles the phone against
his shoulder. Neither party speaks,
yet leagues of fiber-optic lines
exchange their silences.

Thinking of Velázquez

A change comes and I'm changed:
gone are the chows and billowing cloaks;
I cook an egg, or sleep.

My elbow broke the plane
of darkened wall and paw proffered—
the comfort of what's known.

I inked my image out
of snow, and saw what was reversed
in every dwarf and nun:

the black-and-white of news
I never had the mind to mind—
writ larger than the sun.

White-Out

The autumn sky has reasons
which reason does not know:

unstable indices of ice
refer to prints of boots and paws;
Pascal and Thomas Vaughan;
Boötes blocked by clouds.

Muffled hedge and bearded pear
uphold a crystal tent;
beneath the fibrous snow
there must be something more
familiar bearing fruit.

11

On the Blue
Line I overheard
an unknown tongue:

after the storm
Sung celadon
cold water and
a moon
of Shang bronze.

I could not
have been
the person who
you thought
I was.

March Air

The trees are bare
    of leaves, and clothes
dissociate
    across the floor.

I take a card
    and recompose
myself from what
    we call "the world."

The Very Thing

Beneath the names
I never knew
that fairy wand
and devil's bit

refer to the same,
or that the leek
and lily are
so much akin—

moist cells beneath
their paper skin.

II

Drunk with the course of an evening's conversation
and full of what I could only describe as myself,

I turn to the power of rain: dispossession
of all but the hissing of rain on my roof.

III

Even a gesture—
brushing against the sleeve—
is but a signature
of flesh—the flesh itself
another matter.

IV

Want:

the relict thought
once more diverse.

Higher Learning

Caterpillars browse
threads of rotten leaves

and learn by rote
as much as they can eat.

Day and night they inch
along an endless branch

like beetle brows
without an eye below.

The Life of Wood

The name is Wood,
though some would say
I'm living flesh.
You see this scar

across my thumb?
I took a saw
to prune some shrubs
while sucking down

another beer
and never felt
it catch and kick—
but saw the blood.

When we were small
my sister flung
a spitting pan
against my ribs,

which left this pale
and waxy patch
(for weeks I lay
alone in bed).

I am without
profession, but
not quite so dumb
as flames infer:

xyloid, that's
a word which means
the same as wood.
I've tried to graft

another life
to mine and make
the juncture smooth.
But scars outlast

both consciousness
and cause—old facts
initialed in
a valentine,

Atlanta, rings
of time within
electric bulbs;
The Life of Wood.

I lean against
a rake and watch
two contrails cross,
then blow apart;

as I once could—
before I had
to harden from
the center out.

Another Version

Those who think through trees
are slow to take up
that which lies beneath—

past and future trees
of shoot and frittered bark,
the preface and appendices

to tree. Since last we spoke
I've lived alone within
a walnut chiffonier

with no acknowledgments
of debt or sign of giving leave
to loss beyond

the massive walnut tree
that kept my precinct clear
of other growth

through poison in its roots;
indexical, tumultuous,
and toothed. By night

its supple branches burn
starch to sugar—saccharides
which filter to the nut;

and puckered drupes display
in ever blacker shades
collapsing cells within,

softening—as they descend
through stages of decay—
their soap-and-pepper sting.

Rot is sweet, and fruit
is prone to decompose.
I found in what was green

and hard, a dark regret;
in liquefaction, stains
for autocratic wood.

Influence

Smoke gets into everything:
bitter honey,

autumn's distillation, bears
an aftertaste

of cats
and muscatel.

When privet
dominates, hives

disperse in sparks
through private darkness,

filling cells
with evidence of elsewhere:

spores of cockle,
rush, and dock;

contraband,
perfume, and punk.

Even you (asleep
and breathing deeply)

open from the core
to all that you are not.

Hymns for Human Composure

tonight
moons

nod
beyond

reach
of work

or wind-
fall

         below
         all

         want
         only

         off-
         balance-

         sheet
         profits

dry
brains

of osage
orange

crowd
the crowns

of leafless
trees

        corpor-
        eal

        or corp-
        orate

        want
        or need

        want
        or need

The Will

for clouds
a vapor trail

        for birds
        a cup of seed

for night
an eau de nil

        for wrong
        a daub of red

for stone
an acid bath

        for waves
        eroded stone

for rent
a cabin berth

        for heat
        mercuric skin

for lust
a purple cloud

           for song
           a ceiling fan

for seasons past
another round

           for once
           a second chance

The Art of Autobiography

FOR ROBERT ADAMSON IN AUSTRALIA

I

Currawongs
in wattle trees
run a song
from reel to reel

in slow reverse.
What I feel
I felt. Rain
hurtles toward
its source.

II

On work detail at Mount Penang
Training School for Boys, you built a road
to nowhere—bittern in the rain,
addressing stumps and clarts
with half-remembered songs.

Holy on! Holy off!
Learning time from appetite,
you made a half-loaf last
by rolling each pinch back to dough,
or "viper raising" [prison slang].

At night, you read *What Bird Is That?*
before the lights went out.

III

Now, in sight of Lion's Head,
you cut the outboard engine. "Look,
a butcher bird!—which Whiteley gave
the eyes of Baudelaire."

To keep amused, we crush bits
of sandwich bread for bait
and fish for Tutty, cross-eyed cat
of porches, purring on the wharf
in expectation. Checking lines,
you lean across the gunnel and sort
a shadow flock from schools
of substance, jellyfish from cloud;
between them intervenes
a nest of fine white hair.

IV

Further out than we will go,
breakers squander, recompose;
time curls back on time.

V

Take a garfish caught
amidst uncertainties
of early fog
and wrapt in sheets

of Water Leaf
and say what chrome
of Customlines
has faded from its scales.

Distinguish frequencies
of shortwave radios
from the mimicry
of cockatoos.

Explain to those who ask
how white was ever false,
or how to mix
a perfect Whiteley blue.

Then speak of things
that everybody knows.

NOTES & ACKNOWLEDGMENTS

My epigraph is taken from Violette Leduc, *La Bâtarde*, translated by Derek Coltman (Farrar, Straus & Giroux, 1965), 240.

"Aversion": Romans performed rites of aversion in the month of February. According to Jane Ellen Harrison in her *Prolegomena to the Study of Greek Religion*, these rituals involved not the invocation of heavenly spirits but the placation of ghosts.

The following poems are free translations from Greek and Latin: "One," Fragment 11 of Archilochos; "Early Spring," Ode I.4 of Horace; "Distant Warnings," Poem 11 of Catullus.

"The Art of Autobiography": Brett Whiteley (1939–1992) was a prominent Australian artist.

The poems included in this volume have appeared in the following publications: *Boston Review, Bridge, The Canary, Can We Have Our Ball Back, Cello Entry, Chicago Review, Columbia Poetry Review, Conundrum, The Cultural Society, Delmar, Fence, First Intensity, Five Fingers Review, Jacket, Lung, Meanjin, New American Writing, Notre Dame Review, Samizdat, Skanky Possum,* and *Slope.*

Some of these poems were published as a chapbook entitled *Aversion* (Backwoods Broadsides #61). "Cat" appeared as a broadside from the Cultural Society and "Doubtful Weather" as a broadside from the Underwood Reading Series.

ABOUT THE AUTHOR

Devin Johnston is the author of a previous book of poetry entitled *Telepathy* (Paper Bark, 2001) as well as a book of criticism, *Precipitations: Contemporary American Poetry as Occult Practice* (Wesleyan University Press, 2002). From 1995-2000, he served as poetry editor for *Chicago Review*, and with Michael O'Leary, he now directs a small press called Flood Editions. Raised in North Carolina, he currently lives in Saint Louis, Missouri, where he teaches at Saint Louis University.

Library of Congress Cataloging-in-Publication Data

Johnston, Devin.
    Aversions poetry / by Devin Johnston.
        p. cm.
    Includes bibliographical references (p.).
    ISBN 1-890650-16-1 (alk. paper)
    I. Title.
    PS3610.0385A94 2004
    811'.6--dc22

                                    2004011510